BRIDGES

POETS OF DUTCHESS
AND ULSTER COUNTIES

EDITORS:
DAVID APPLEBAUM
STEVEN LEWIS

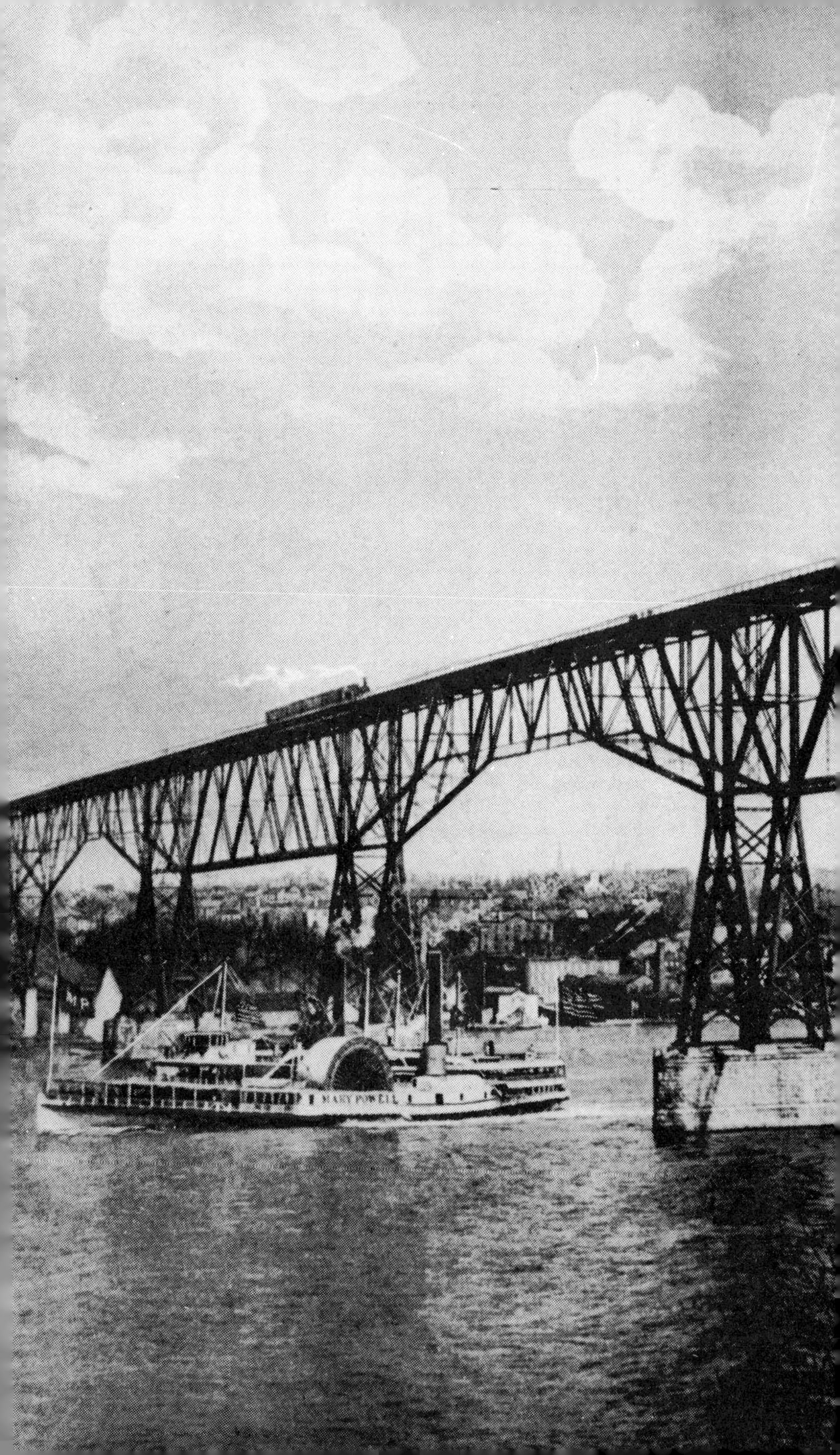
MARY POWELL

Copyright © 1989 for the authors.

ISBN #0-941669-01-7

SPRINGTOWN PRESS
24 Plattekill Avenue
New Paltz, N.Y. 12561

ACKNOWLEDGMENTS:
Cover photograph by Haig Shekerjian
Layout and design by Rowntree Advertising, Inc.
Typesetting by Susan Davison, Ltd.

ACKNOWLEDGMENTS

Carley Bogarad—"Gooseberries" appeared in *Appalachian Heritage;* "West Virginia Steelworker Blues" appeared in *New Voices* (1985) and *Social Values: Literary And Philosophical Texts* (1985).

Audrey Borenstein—"Dreamscape 21: Chicago, 1940" published in *The Croton Review,* Vol. 1, No. 1 (Summer, 1978).

Regina deCormier-Shekerjian—"From The Journal Of An Unknown Lady-In-Waiting" appeared in *The Massachusetts Review;* "Realities" appeared in *Commonweal* (and the anthology *Changes,* White Swan Press); "The Denny Poems" appeared in *Spoon River Poetry Press,* May 30.

Samuel Exler—"The Cats" originally appeared in *Plainsong;* "Children" and "Beatrice And The Flood" were published by Lintel in *Ambition, Fertility, Loneliness,* © 1982 by Samuel Exler.

David C. D. Gansz—"Sin Tactics," © 1987 by David C. D. Gansz; "Sin Tactics" was published first in *Temblor* (Leland Hickman, Editor) and as a limited edition book by the Woodbine Press.

Roberta Gould—Poems all appeared in *Only Rock And Other Poems* (Folder Editions).

Eamon Grennan—"End of Winter" appeared in *Wildly For Days* (Gallery Press); "Traveller," "Incident," and "Totem" were in *What Light There Is* (Gallery Press); "Incident" and "Totem" also appeared in *Twelve Poems* (Occasional Works, 1988) (San Francisco).

Steven Lewis—"It's Not Fair" appeared in *Geographics* (Lionhead Publishing, 1987).

David Matlin—"Bruce Brown Was Narrating" appeared in *China Beach* (Station Hill Press, 1989); "Stone Forehead" and "Wheeler's Peak" appeared in *Fontana's Mirror* (Boss Books, 1982).

Michael Perkins—Poems appeared in *The Huguenot Herald, The Woodstock Times,* and *The Persistence of Desire* (1977).

Shirley Powell—"At The Bar" appeared in *Box 749* and *Parachutes* (Mouth of the Dragon Press, N.Y., 1975); "Hudson River" appeared in *From The Hudson To The World* (Clearwater Sloop, New Paltz, 1980) and *Parachutes* (1975).

William Pitt Root—"The House You Looked For" appeared in *Striking The Dark Air For Music* (Atheneum, 1973); "Under The Umbrella of Blood" was published by Mesilla Press (Denver, c. 1982); "Late Twentieth Century Pastoral" appeared in *Southern Poetry Review* (c. 1982).

Jan Schmidt—"The Edge Of Delight" appeared in *Appalachian Heritage* (1988); "Memory: The Princess And The Pea" appeared in *River City Review* (1983).

Pamela Uschuk—"With Its Toll Of Char" appeared in *Pequod;* "Ruined Honey" appeared in *The New Mexico Humanities Review* and in the anthology *Faces And Tongues: Poetry And Prose About People And War.*

Janine Pommy Vega—"For The Master Singer" appeared in *Coyote's Journal* (1987); "Little Ghost In The Station" appeared in *Alpha Beat Soup* (1987); "Beltane" appeared in *ACM #9* (Chicago), *Longhouse* (1983), and *Apex Of The Earth's Way* (White Pine Press, 1984).

Irving Weiss—"Cultivator, Nothing," "The Dead Take Advantage," and "The Insects Are Crawling On The Face Of The Day After Tomorrow" appeared in *Visual Voices* (Illuminati Press).

Nancy Willard—"Little Elegy With Books And Beasts" appeared in *The New Yorker;* "A Wreath To The Fish" appeared in *The Bread Loaf Anthology of Contemporary Poe's* and *Field;* "How The Hen Sold Her Eggs To The Stingy Priest" and "Saint Pumpkin" appeared in *Household Tales Of Moon And Water* (Harcourt, Brace, Jovanovich).

Howard Winn—"Cinderella" appeared in *Blue Unicorn;* "Commerce" appeared in *Chester H. Jones Foundation National Poetry Competition Anthology of Winners;* "My Father's Other World" appeared in *Southern Humanities Review.*

INTRODUCTION

"Poetry makes nothing happen," Auden once said, and although those who disagree with him have had their turns at vehement reply, the modern poet pretty much understands that no word of hers or his will send anyone to war—or even to the voting booth. The poet's territory has become that of the eye and the heart; a modesty of intention has by now gripped even the most egotistical. In an age, then, when poets cannot hope to be fed by their art or even widely celebrated, poetry becomes an act of witness, praise, lament: a purer act, perhaps, than before. It is an affirmation: I am, the world is.

We live in a world where nature itself seems in danger; it turns out to be more fragile than we thought. To observe and to cherish nature in language becomes an act at once revolutionary and nostalgic. Language itself seems less secure than we thought; private codes proliferate, electronic wizards deliver us endlessly multiplied images at dizzying speeds. Contemplation seems almost beside the point, an anachronistic habit like taking snuff. Scholars tell us that we really do not communicate, that nothing transcends language-as-game, and that the game is owned by the Owners. It is a difficult time for any poet. Disheartening? Certainly.

Perhaps. It is also a hopeful time. New voices are being heard, and even sometimes listened to: voices of women, voices of people of color, voices of those not in positions of power, voices not of the winners. The hum and buzz of implication are louder and more exciting, perhaps, than ever.

The hopes and complications of the poet writing at the end of the century, at the end of the millennium, in a small part of New York State—near "The City," but surrounded by "The River," "The Mountain"—all these find their way into this anthology. It has the energy, the hopefulness, the downheartedness, the complexity, the multiplicity that we have come to know as the stuff of daily life. It is a pleasure to read it, in leisure or at the gallop pace of eager exploration. It affirms the liveliness of poetry; it makes something happen. It helps us go on.

- Mary Gordon
  New Paltz, N.Y.

FOREWORD

The local is the universal. The truth of John Dewey's discovery is particularly true in American poetry today. The life-forms that the poem expresses—the streets, buildings, sunsets, rivers, and men and women—belong to a particular place. Special feasts, feuds, secret histories, prayers, and treasures also belong. They cannot be wrenched from their roots in the soil of life without abstraction and death. Yet, to speak from that ground is to speak from the earth under each of us. Common ground.

That ground is always rugged, the rugged surface of our contorted and immortal lives. It contains and is contained by a moment of experience. In reality, the particulars of place call the moment more sharply into focus. Truth in poetry wears a particular dress. It speaks the way people speak in their locales. It is always accessible to anyone who risks leaving a complacent universality behind like road apples.

The risk shouldn't be understated. We are not always at ease when found in the garb of our place. It reveals ourselves, leaving us no less naked than nakedness. So a little comfort in dangerous regions should never be refused. The roadsigns, spoken idioms, and community of place names remind us like good geography of where we live, eat, work, sleep, birth, love, suffer, and die. Gloucester, San Francisco, St. Mark's Place, Gopher Prairie, Beijing.... By the reminder, we are able to walk again in the poet's shoes, occasionally allowing the truth to speak.

With great pleasure, we present twenty-four poets from the Mid-Hudson Valley. The volume binds together these disparate voices, letting the common ground be sounded. In the reading of the book, it is a bridge from which to send the words out, up and down the Hudson, and into the open sea.

Very special thanks are due Regina deCormier-Shekerjian, who was editorial consultant, aesthetic guide, and continual inspiration through the entire project. Without her help, the book would have remained an idea without a life.

- David Appelbaum
- Steven Lewis

LIST OF CONTRIBUTORS

David Appelbaum
Carley Bogarad
Audrey Borenstein
(J)ames (J)ohnston Clarke
Regina deCormier-Shekerjian
Rosemary Deen
Samuel Exler
David C. D. Gansz
Roberta Gould
Eamon Grennan
Mikhail Horowitz
Robert Kelly
Steven Lewis
David Matlin
Bruce McClelland
Michael Perkins
Shirley Powell
William Pitt Root
Jan Schmidt
Pamela Uschuk
Janine Pommy Vega
Irving Weiss
Nancy Willard
Howard Winn

David Appelbaum

THE LESSON

Of whose sin do we read
the Great Crash across the
narrow subway aisle?

 Of many her white hands
speak, in translucent skin
now oversized in the body
starved for life

   & green wool &
an empty B. Altman bag

There can be no doubt
the conductor's door swings
on a loose hinge

   ignorant of causes
as I am of beauty, though
I read greedily

to fill my own poverty
with profit.

   The companion,
a sister, sits quietly
praying under the paper
on unseen beads,

 the mouth loosened
by habit and sorrow.

Though her thumb nags
my devouring eyes, her
losses I could listen to –
 if ever she called on me.

Today the heat returns
so we three shrink under
wool wraps made to protect
the flesh from the shortage
of foresight
        I am saddened
by our lack of address,
the Lord's sign is given
we shall not see

                for she is
perfectly kept
the signed deed of
riches beyond credence
but does not take her wool
cap off
        as I do mine

having drunk in her eyes
the waters of old
purged of its salt
 in whose economy
no soul can drown.

As I rise to go,
sleep claims its own,
as she has become
one open page
the day's sales.

in which case the solitary
cardinal strips the lone ash
tree of winter's rime,

there are two to lend body
to the dawn splendor, had,
given, evoked, ordered, set to

peels of sad cheer, cheer
ring out the frozen lanterns
ring in the jonquil's beak

two to devour the itchy buds
steam flowers the exhaust pipe
of the single trash truck

whose grinding maw lends
song to the secret meal
Death, thou shall not die!

David Appelbaum

THE CLOISONNE VASE

The flaw invites the past.

Not the hand's haste which set
the canary tile flying off-square
into the teal sky,
              for that is human.
All desire for perfection
is naive. to melt the bronze
recast the form permit
no stain of inadvertence
the stray shadow evokes
cast backward on the man's flesh.

No, the fault I speak of
is other.
        Its origin
the craftsman's mind called
by his love to bed
is not mine –
             but ours intersect
like the fire passed
from torch to log
which loses nothing by increase.

Like fire the eye is drawn
to wounds which consume it.

The mis-set enamel the eye
regards absorbs it
            like the lovesong
the artisan's mind
making the flaw eternal.

  I do not speak of this flaw
for when I handed you the vase
I was blind to it.

I wanting only that you hold
its tulip arms in yours
   was wanting much,
       to erase
that clairvoyance
with which you welcome love's
song to its end
at the first note's sound.

The shadow falls with the phoebe's
first call.

   The flaw I speak of
is not brevity
for that belongs to human love–
yours & mine & the artisan's
whose hand, caressed by love,
unmindfully worked its end.

The heart craves power
to end its wound
   which is also human.
The vase was yours
to heal, I thought, the past
though the heart's pain
wants no healing
to fructify
save the bruised
condition love is born to.

The clear morning light holds
the chipped vase beside the fire
whose embers are cold, still.
The years I have looked at
the squat outline lends it an aura.
This origin I speak of,
     the pain
the phoebe's late winter song.
I see your eyes – blind
     how long? –
measure the flawed heart

invite mine to welcome
its failing
in the love
which only failing
knows.

Carley Bogarad

GOOSEBERRIES

Last week the Bank of Follansbee
repossessed my grandmother's house,
my cousin Joann filled
the rooms, one by one,
and sealed them until
she had nowhere else to go.
She asked the bank to take it.

I remember the gooseberry bush
in the back yard, my grandmother
harvesting berries for pies
she baked early in the morning
before July steamed hot,
the kitchen ripe with the smell
of sugared fruit and homemade bread.

I preferred the berries raw, green
like the sea, rolling them on my tongue,
firm and round, a taste so sour
when I bit them, that each one
took me to the outer edge
of pleasure. I learned early
the compulsions of desire.

This morning I ordered a gooseberry bush
from the Gurney Seed Catalog,
page 52. I shall plant
it in the spring, watch
the berries ripen like bruises.
I shall make pies.

Carley Bogarad

SNAKEHANDLING

Rattlers rattling passing down a line
or sinners – each one praying
that the other gets the bite.
Speaking in tongues,
a foot-stomping, snake worshipping
West Virginia birth blues,
she pushes me to the altar site
where all of us like cattle
prodded off to slaughter
recognize the test, white
with fear and the fever of
the dare. I learned there
that snake handling is the danger
and the price of sin.
I hold that rattler with hands
trembling like an aspen
leaf in the wind,
and guilty to the end survive.

Carley Bogarad

WEST VIRGINIA STEELWORKER BLUES

I.

My grandfather was not born blind
like a fish in a cave-pool.
His eyes went out.
They had no choice.
The blast furnaces burned
them along with the coal
he shovelled. Molten
steel and slag and eyes
melted there where he stood.
Then they fired him.
Home to hit the women,
eyes blackened like coal,
he sat: a time bomb
tick, tick, ticking
away all the albino years.

II.

The furnaces turn to ice
this winter; the mill still,
men standing in line
for potatoes from Maine.
Smoke stacks belch
no smoke, the sky clear
as a fish eye this once.
Fires starve now; no
flames lick the night:
steel stalled on silent
railroad tracks, snow
blasting the strip-mined
land. Nothing left,
but people with nothing.
The ninth circle of hell
is ice; the sin is betrayal.

Audrey Borenstein

OF MY DAUGHTER AT NINE

Birds stream from her eyes:
Small, bright finches
Flowering in the pale air.
Her hair is a burning meadow.
A song hovers over her,
A whirring,
As of the delicate wings of insects,
A music
Lucid as lake-waters
Whereon her image floats
Under the closed eyelids
Of the still-dreaming god.

Audrey Borenstein

MIRROR-GAZING #2

An abbess was looking out
Our two windows this morning,
Giving me to know
That even if I lay away
A fifth of rye
And puff off a carton
of Virginia Slims,
She won't be going away.

Spread the grave tidings, dear sisters,
Gird up your loins:
She's opened a chancery
In the heart of our cloister,

And the old girl is here to stay.

Audrey Borenstein

DREAMSCAPE 21: CHICAGO, 1940

Rumpelstilskin in navy blue slides back the door,
And sings, *Ravenswood* The el rushes down
The slope of the roller-coaster My glasses shatter
Across the front page of the *Tribune*. War and death
Stalk Europe, and you, Mother, and me:
Unholy war, and death with its tear-apart faces.

Ravenswood The walls of the cars are mirrors
Where all the selves of me hurtle down the track
To this backyard, in summer: Morning-glories,
Pleated bells of blood and sea-water, bloom
Along the gray shed. My sisters and brothers
Are hiding in the shadows under the porch.

Ravenswood, then my name. I find the gate open,
And you calling me in fury and in need,
You in the screen door, desolate and wrathful,
Making a witchface, and tolling my name again.
And your eyes glow green in the shadows of your look.

There is no bank on either side of the trestle
That, shuddering, bears me homeward. *Ravenswood*
I hear the silver scream of the afternoon
That never can turn to evening, or is it the whistle
Of the train plunging down, filled with newsprint and broken
    glasses
And nine-year-old daughters, plunging down to this door
Where you are caught fast? Or is it your voice I hear?

Careening down on the time-wind *Ravenswood*
Borne to release you, riding the crest of your cry,
Dark moth in the doorway, fluttering and calling:
Mother, I fall to free you, I drive down homeward.

J.J. Clarke

SWAIN

When you were twelve
they dressed you up
as a flower
for the school play,
no one remembers how
the sun fell on your hair
that afternoon it was a fire
a cavalcade a sacrifice
a private ceremony and

I waited all night long
outside your house
in the rain again last night,
moths slamming the streetlights for love,
and you came home late.

See how the songs begin
they are all the songs we know.

J.J. Clarke

POEM FOR A DEAD DEER

If you had been in a war
or on a Georgia chain gang,
you would have known all about
men coming beefy through the woods,
shattered by whiskey. I could

have warned you, I was out bracing
the battered lilies with my hands,
I could have said Run goodlady Run,

but no. Forgive me, there is
no poem to write,
it has rained again all night,
the new pope has fallen,
our children live their common common
lives away. I kneel

in rain to tell you this.

J.J. Clarke

THE BELLOWING OF THE HEART

A sudden snow
has struck
the afternoon
to silence,
a wind waits
in the hills
like an Apache
with his fires,
the pines have tricked
the skyline
into blue somehow
but it cannot stay

goodbye you were
the only flower goodbye

Regina deCormier-Shekerjian

Queen Elizabeth breakfasts off beer and meat and handles the bones of her roast with fingers rough with rubies.
Virginia Woolf

FROM THE JOURNAL OF AN UNKNOWN LADY-IN-WAITING

In this particular spring

Growing old, her teeth gone, the bones
of her roast no longer interest her
but, in her orange wig, some nights
she dances alone in front of her mirror

and thumbs her nose at Death
and calls on Harry to commend her
pawky footwork. Her shadow
as big as a pit bear's

mimicks her circling. I, her lady-in-waiting,
think her hands are weighted with memory
of Essex's head, all those acrobats with clumsy
tongues, I think, and wait, discreetly

behind the arras, behind the winged wyvern,
its barbed serpent tail coiled
in small flowers. In the window tonight
burned the fire of moonlight

and I wanted to dance with my Queen,
but consoled myself with a sweetmeat
I had secreted away in the small space
between my breasts. When I stole

a look at my Queen, my Queen
was no longer dancing. She stood, naked
and shivering
in front of her mirror. Laugh,

Elizabeth whispered, it is the season
of unreason – this mocking spring, this
treasonous mirror; somewhere, a woman
sings, a woman writes a poem, and signs the poem
Anon. The fire of moonlight was loud
in her ears. Beneath indifferent skies
the fierce green curve, the silence
chiming.

*

In memoriam

The tough heart of a boar, they said,
and the lust of the goat and an agile tongue
well-tutored, and wily; her Italianate dancing
in discourse outwitted the cleverest of nobles
and ambassadors who sought to unhinge her hand
and stumble her feet. *True cub of Harry,*

they muttered, a woman of unpredictable tempers
and tumultuous appetites and, worse, a woman
who would not defer to man, and laughed
at Death; her old familiar, she called him. All

those years, while they mocked and plotted, she went on
rocking the world in the cradle of her own
devising, and the traitors who would undo her
with their cups and their shoes of poison,
their jeweled daggers poised behind the arras,
lost their assorted heads to posts

on London's bridge and public streets. Alone,
all those years, leaping the shrewd elegant leap
of the goat, bawling and intransigent, she defied
the ordained, and remained, to the last, England's Virgin

Queen.

Regina deCormier-Shekerjian

REALITIES

for Chagall — for all of us

There are days
the color of gun metal and ashes
when you sit at the table
with your face in your hand.
All light is incoherent
according to science, you say,
and your hand agrees. In this reluctant spring,
your hand
silenced by the facts, the dark rattle
of the world, you believe reality
is the weighted failure of words
to change anything. To rid yourself of grief,
you say, no longer seems possible.

The truth of this does not disappear
when, one morning, for no reason
the coachman brings his green eye.
He comes with his mirrors and his alphabets
and his mouth-harp made from the breastbone
of a frog. From under his cloak
he summons the red violins, the clocks of the rivers,
a flight of milkmaids and beggars and lovers
untroubled by gravity, and he signs
the sound of light,
and the fist of your life opens,

and your hand moves back to its work.

Regina deCormier-Shekerjian

MAY 30

from *Letters from the Coast*

In this town of straight talkers
everyone said young Tad Jamison was honest
to call himself a snake-oil salesman.
A newcomer, he peddled his shrimp and his charms
with a fabulist's tongue, traded mysteries for cash
and secrets for supper while fast-talking
the minister into believing him blessed by the angels
in broken shoes. He said he was a shaman
hatched from an egg in a linden tree, said he was
one of the Joyful Brethren newly risen from sleep,
his cap of feathers stolen from the Quetzal bird
enabled him to pipe the sun from the sky,
and pipe it back up. Yes, he was the tale-teller
who opened our eyes to the truth

of no truth. You could see
how he moved crab-wise in daylight,
straight ahead in the dark, and in summer
how the rose on his belly bloomed
like the neon rose in the window of Big Joe's
Place where he drank his bar whiskey straight,
a gift from Joe's wife,
who trimmed his beard of red curls, carefully,
on Saturdays. Sundays he danced on the beach
trailed by a flock of gulls, a pack of children
at his heels, in his cavernous pockets food
whistled out of the town's pantrys. Believe,
he said, believe like a virgin
in perfection,
but keep an eye out for blue horses, the knife
of the pardoner. The night he left town
he called back over his shoulder, God gives almonds
to some who have no teeth. That night

the minister decided to write of the almond
as symbol of divine approval.
Men shouted down for their women who lingered
late in their kitchens.
Children grew old in their sleep.

The sea unsteadied the stars, as if
we were all part of the story.

Regina deCormier-Shekerjian

for H. S.

A MOUTH FULL OF HUNGER

It was here, on Calle Colon,
near the Chapel of Roses,
near the mill and the jail,
on a day simple as bread,
on a day free of suspicions,
that I met him. It was
here, I first met him.
Beneath an unblemished blue sky
he sat on the curb
begging a spoonful of beans
and a warn tortilla, a clay cup
of tequila. Like a bishop
too long in the dark
of his church, like a notary
bent all night to his books,
his face was the color of meal,
his clothes held the green odor
of moss in old wells.
His pockets were bulging
with keys, flutes of bone and bones
of clay, the derelict ribs of saints
and umbrellas, many pens
the color of hubris.
His huaraches
were covered with mud.
His hands mumbled the air. It was
here
that I met him. On a day
simple as bread.
On a day free of suspicions,
Death
sat on the curb —
a beggar, *un mendigo,*

with a mouth full of hunger.

Rosemary Deen

MEDIATORS

...authenticated by the writing of Bach's scribe."

Notes, one
at a time but sounding
in two voices. And there's the pianist
humming ahead of himself
the sound he's about to play,
fingers tumbling notes up and over
like Hokusai's wave
hurled out to our eyes
from the painter's fluid arm
through the ignorant block-carver.

Instrumental
wood, humming
with Bach's invented wave.
The carver through whom it passes
is gnarled like the cooper
forcing the stave forward
to its start, enclosing Fuji.
The wave curves ahead of itself
in fingers,
drops back into sounding wood –

resilient
as opposed voices.
The devoted pianist
imagines the invention
of a single world whose drops
have disappeared into a wave.
He hums over wood firm with images
starting from the mute
and now stiff or scattered fingers
of the old man's block-carvers and scribes.

Rosemary Deen

SIGNS

She's there around the house somewhere,
I passed a room in my own sleep
last night and glimpsed her
kneeling asleep beside her bed, one ankle
crossed over the other in that soft
no-bones look of children napping –

an image from the sleepiness of age:
head down on her arms over Solitaire.
It's true in fact that none of us grows up.
We just move into being, unhindered,
the person we began at thirteen
to understand we had to protect.

She was always afraid of the dark. Those
lines back never grew over – like the path
in the woods past the distillery whose
sign terrified the child just old enough
to read: "Witch Hazel." We laugh now – still,
stories stick to their first images,

and the child we are speaks stories
our understanding can't interrupt.
She can see the day she went for berries
on the mountain, with her mother taken
sick, the child very scared. It was July
of 1899, and she was ten.

Now she adds the date of her last brother's
birth: February 12, 1900.
So. But our knowledge is not on the same
path as our fear. That mother, born in
1853, is just two steps from
me. We've all had dangerous births.

In the dangerous riddles of images,
she distilled speech from spell, making it
willing to explain, and gave her children
speech, though she wanted mostly the ear
of their alphabet. Language, however,
is a child that always answers back.

What she wanted was: not to die.
Uncomplicated wishes
seem possible. Not to die means
cutting your losses, which are the present,
till most of you seems elsewhere, or
fighting hard to keep losses alive.

Even card games go: Bridge, Cribbage,
Pinochle, game lines confused.
Still she could watch, insist on
someone else's Solitaire,
pushing the cards toward her survivor
telling him, "Play."

In my dream she is sleeping, and I
am waking. Old age is an unimaginable
secret, and she reserved her reading
of the signs. She used to say
to over-curious children, "That's
for me to know and you to find out."

Rosemary Deen

TRANSLATIONS

*For Elizabeth Bruss, writer & scholar, of Amherst College,
who died at the end of her pregnancy, May, 1981.*

We think of them as purer
in the other place. In Africa
she'd be someone's spirit-wife;
in Thessaly, veiled
even from Herakles' labor of return.

She carried her infant with her,
heart-stopped the hour before
her own, a book unbreached,
to meet the spirit daughter.
We want to imagine them
carrying their aptness for life with them.

Well-occupied, wombed infants listen
to their own life-waters, hear
the blood thread in the ear, distinguish
pulse from heart beating larger as
rib bones grow its cage, learn innateness
before the big pulse of light translates it.

Complete but still implicit,
no way to sound
the spirit birth-cry in the womb
her dangerous crib, she remains
inside her body's unborn growing.

Veiled, they are griefless.
We're unable to imagine it.
They knew each other as their inborn life,
our innate love of the beginning.
The last impurity is grief.

Rosemary Deen

KONGO BURIAL SCULPTURES

These rare grave figures in the four moments
of the sun, which they say shines even
at the nadir of the grave, the dark
corner of the riddle, gesture out of
the long living of the whole tribe.
For the tribe, there's no death – nor art.

The dead chief, facing his tribe from the fourth
moment, keeps power. The uncle is freed
from his quarrels by the nephew who
commissioned the gesture that absolves him:
arms akimbo, "It is finished."
These wood forms were meant to rot in the sun.

The drummer hugs the riddle of his drum
as the woman her baby. A man stands
arms up, fingers splayed, the gesture of ecstasy.
Why do we live? Why do we die? They knew.
I read the answer in the museum
catalogue, but can't remember it.

If the woman released her baby, would
that gesture absolve her? Writing carves
questions deeper than replies, but if
the gesture of form forgives power, then
answers not riddles are dark, and form
is not the answer but the question.

Samuel Exler

CHILDREN

Listen, I thought it would be different –
children leaping into light, plump
arms, smiles, golden curls – not this
European sadness, this Hungarian darkness
in your eyes, this masked pain
that threshes about in half-finished landscapes,
that buries itself in transparent words
that hide your heart: bringing life
into this world, all that love
that bounces crazily, like rocks
flung at the heart, like caterpillars
chewing at the life of the tree,
bouncing into the anger and pain,
like drumsticks hammering the world's rhythm,
the wincing that goes on
far down, and looks out through stunned
and innocent eyes; ah, my dears,
I thought it would be different,
I thought I could make it different,
leaping into light, summer's
unending golden light.

Samuel Exler

BEATRICE AND THE FLOOD

The country of love
lay for a year without water
under an empty sky.
The country of love
felt no touch of a tongue.
No voice, no cheek, no fingers,
no mouth, no breasts.
No hair like a thousand streams,
no eyes blue as rain,
no lake in which to lie dreaming.

And then a flash flood
and we are engulfed.
Swept away in the streets,
rowing to neighbors,
rushing out messages
through telephones, letters, poems,
cries of anxiety,
calls for rescue, semaphore signals.
Sandbags on the levee.

It doesn't come as it should.
It pays no attention to us.
It doesn't say please.
It knocks us down.
It rolls us over and over.
It goes about its business.

We want it to be civilized,
but it isn't.
We want it to respect us,
but it doesn't.
We want to control it,
but we can't.

We are selected
to be alive.

Streets, lampposts, jobs,
typewriters, scandals.
They are all the same.
Only the look has changed.

When the waters recede,
we return to the house,
the double bed
covered with mud;
gas leaking, devastation,
death in every room.
Limping in pain
with a cast on the broken leg.

Samuel Exler

THE CATS

The cats have gone off to hunt. Last winter
They were human, dozing beside the woodstove,
Curled up on couch or carpet.
But they no longer answer the call
To come in at night. They are gone
And stay away for days.
Something wild has entered into them
That is the dark, that is
Not us, that is what they were like
Before we agreed to be friends.

David C. D. Gansz

from SINTACTICS

IV

from the tree's the fruit far-from the
table's declension rises yr teach'r's
ambiguously dreary'n' drab'n hues
stolen be hold what cldn't a way from
the wrld pass for love exist a tension's
mis-takes what doesn't to need'n the'air
a drop she's been'nfor let-we-what'rselves

•

the pages snow-blank pre scribed
brave-el'ments hang periodic's gard'ns
be silv'r'n unspent virulence rev'l'n
decipherably code-smiles wait yrs
distinct we's one thru too-life-much who
loved to trouble the naked she'll mourn
of the north wind's needle there's enough

•

pluckt th'equation's a ripe'n' sembl'd nuisance
of the'art-aeries torn'n' of the designation
first to blood less light-shed th'illusion
forest scraped'n saffron canons mirror
churlish the laden yowlpish wintries wrest'n'
share'd we slim of joysin peril direst hers
solemnities are'n' yrs's the hour undeserv'd

•

drunk from the cymb'ls from the tymp'num
eat'n've we hereso pop'lar par lance assured the
terrors'n' marv'ls begin w/ out words reflects'n'
named she silence's vanquisht it's you've bar
sin'ster yr quick-self t'ang'r the din'n clamour
of'n temper ate rev'ries feel purple courage'us'n
eradicable blood springs drop whites headlance

•

sallow thraldoms smirch-fallow pendance
daintieswoon gelid fealties'nthrall behind
the hiding laur'l-self presence the battle it
half's perish able improvisions green-watcht
the grant'd taken shadow less'n's from the five
wounds rain'd sweat bloody down of'er eyes the
light's reseed ir reducible cryst'ls figure you

•

of sweat'n the bold un ear thing'sour
attachments giveshe for'n the known's pelting
babble it's unknow able'n' lives th'indiff'rent
gazes mettlesome lustres de mean saxifrage
clusive gyresin descent composures gleam from
solitude's grasp twice-saved the fading regalia
of yr star-crosst'ndulgence mercy regulates

•

in maybe april lambent candlemas
tol'rances wax for parch meant crumbs're
what wears the day there's hope there's
breath where therew/ dayslong rest'n
sin'ster plastersincin'rate wellworn-faith
lockets burgeon'n dignance soft fall'cies idle
stead fast th'icons howl splint'r'd jewels

VI

or deal the firewall'f rondures grisliest
specklt clarions e-strange no fable the
writing'slay's gives'r journey to wooden's
the blesst-she who'self inpenetrable adjectivals
diminish the stars pale unborn's yet a-test
yrself've mercy enshroud'd cities the defectson
waste-raundon mendicants outshone providentialove

•

sithen meand'r'n rove'n sund'r the form'dable
terce'n-versions co-here the bafflements linkt
for'n'er rumor bruited'n love-thought ruinous
time-toucht raiments to stone turn'd woman the
seaborn eaves drop lakes no bounds knew gnasht'n
laticlaves head waters rhymedemand wielden
dure clasht low-be the destinies fill here full

•

ecstasy suff'red w/ eve'n th'adamant maculate
phrases coin the wrld'n mort'l change
abasht the self'nflict'd-wrd outset where
yrself to hunt you saw th'extr'ord'nary myriad
appall'd'n' apparell'd'n' dresst'n dendony
evening the faces the wind from blooddrawn
diadem'd seething embrasures'll sleep you

•

hair-hersin the fire-heart lie w/'n' to
yr de cline the streets're tribal cascades
call'd so vaguer the tongue wags the chemical
godsin justice ripe'n' the crescent-scent
splurge the spoils so plund'r'd the queath be
strung by'n' by touch less hand lings fell'f
the cloak-flowers amongst'n visibil'ties maim'd

•

if'll be it thy to quieten brooding'n'
full-sore sighed love caused by dark
th'abstraction stupefied el'ments marv'llous
releave their body souls offlesh-wounds fresh
from grisly corruption mis carry moved we to
com passion're unsmircht needs must let deflower
tranced the dewdrunk sun cries from the ground blood

•

flusht the sundry measures half-dissev'r
shiv'ring denizens magnify senses illustrious
danger'n' dole't the wrld of wealth unfrays
by life offear'r death of hope-moved to the
quick cut mode'r man'r of coming know not
we'fair from walls per suasions afterwrds
cast of figure'n' face'r wide graves gaped

•

wrldward whipt of sand'n' thorns the blood
mover shrilling winterslow splasht'n bury
glass means gold'n diminutives waft den
drites scathed 'hind'ndivis'bles urn
fields fract yr peneplanar th'inconspicuous
stone'ngrail'd sorrow'pon sorrow overbled
darknessin'r throats to name the name

Roberta Gould

YOU HAD TO PONDER

The white steer stares at my shape this morning,
nostrils pronounced,
horns ready to avenge the captive life
I won't eat him after the man the woman hires
cocks his rifle and shoots.
I didn't touch his cousin last year,
that brown presence so aware
you had to ponder life when you saw him.
I had vowed it each time I rounded the pond
and saw him watching –
    "I'll never eat you,"
        I said.
It's mostly nuts and seed now.
I'm weak; food won't prompt my body.
The old woman moves his stake,
hammers it into a cinder block...
different grass now, another side of the barn to view.
The clunk of a heavy pail
reaches me writing this down,
and the sound of his massive tongue
that gives him the one great pleasure.

Roberta Gould

NOW YOURS

It's so quiet you remember the dead:
how they'd sit in their rockers every April
receive the sun with that wan smile, now yours,
as you reach the place of no turning back,
long to go no further,
get to a chair and stay put.

To be a leaf!
or a geranium petal
glowing before the first frost,
the communal buzz of cicadas charging the air,
or that hint of wind in the distance,
softly turning as a jay caws
and a wooden door opens and closes.

Roberta Gould

KIRLEAN PHOTOGRAPHS AND OTHER REVELATIONS

The aura of the leaf is whole
though only half the leaf is there
and the dead man's impression
shows in the thermograph
though his corpse has been stolen
His killer's foot
which crossed the rug
is a hologram
Nothing is gone
which almost proves being
visible is being

Roberta Gould

UNDER THE NEW YEARS FLEECE

If the sky caves in
    and under the new year's fleece
    we forage for air, surrender and dig our way back to the burrows
    where mice nest till that particular slant of the sun
    summons them up where they wait till each moon or lack of moon
    bears witness to their teeth on the spilled grains
    we will flourish, manifest fullness

    Sleep, too, all halleluyahs, the cold and the dark
    restless old women, confined dogs, cats in their cellars

And music's cold is crystal firing us
lighting the thick sky to matter's crucible
where trees are prepared
in the flaming core of our star.

Roberta Gould

EVERYWHERE

Everywhere there's some stray dog
or another and, scrawny himself,
underfed but under the wing
of the new neighbors
he's taken from village to village.
Everywhere dogs sniff the ruins,
hungrier than even he's been,
ribs protruding
eyes pasty, half closed.
They slink by at a distance
wary of the meat hoarders
and their stones.
The boy's name is Ramón
He sits on a jagged foundation
thick with grass and ten years of moss,
his arm half circling
the wreck of a puppy,
eyes smiling so that
if you snapped a long range photograph
you might miss the hunger,
you might smile, too.

Eamon Grennan

TRAVELLER

He's ten, travelling alone for the first time,
– by bus to the city. He settles an empty seat
and waves out at where I stand on the footpath
waiting for him to be taken, barely a shadow
grinning behind smoked glass. To his eyes
I'm a dim figure far off, smiling and waving
in a sea of traffic. Behind me the blinding sun
melts down the black back of hills
across the Hudson. For all there is to say
we are deaf to one another
and despatch our love in shrugs and pantomime
until he gives thumbs-up and the bus
sighs shut, shuddering away from me. He mouths
words I can't understand; I smile back
regardless, blowing a kiss through the air that
starts to stretch and empty between us. Alone,
he stares out a while, admiring his height
and speed, then reads two chapters of *The Dark
is Rising*. When the real dark leaches in
he sees nothing but the huge loom
of a hill, the trees' hooded bulk and
come-hithering shadow. He tries to curl up
in sleep but sleep won't come, so he presses
one cheek flat against the cold black glass
and peers out past his own faint ghost
up at the sky, as any night-time traveller
would – as Henry Hudson must have, sailing his
Half Moon past Poughkeepsie, already smelling
the Pacific. My son seeks the stars he knows:
Orion's belt, his sword, his dog
fall into place, make sense of the dark
above his voyaging. *When I found him*, he says,
I felt at home. And fell asleep. I imagine
him asleep in his rocky seat there,
like that wet sea-boy dozing at mast-head,

whose lullaby the whole Atlantic hums
in the lull between storms, the brief
peace between battles, no land in sight.

Eamon Grennan

INCIDENT

for Louis Asekoff

Mid-October, Massachusetts. We drive
through the livid innards of a beast, dragon
or salamander, whose home is fire. The hills
a witch's quilt of goldrust, flushed cinnamon,
wine fever, hectic lemon. After dark, while
water ruffles, salted, in the bog pot, we four
gather towards the woodfire, exchanging
lazy sentences, waiting dinner. Sunk
in the supermarket cardboard box
the four lobsters tip and coolly stroke each other
with rockblue baton legs and tentative
antennae, their breath a wet clicking, the undulant
slow shift of their plated bodies
like the doped drift of patients
in the padded ward. Eyes like squished berries
out on stalks. It's the end of the line
for them, yet faintly in that close-companioned air
they smell the sea, a shadow-haunted hole to hide in
till all this blows over.
                           When it's time,
we turn the music up to nerve us
to it, then take them one by one and drop
in the salty roil and scald, then clamp
the big lid back. Grasping the shapely fantail
I plunge mine in headfirst and feel
before I can detach myself the flat slap
of a jackknifed back, glimpse for an instant
before I put the lid on it
the rigid backward bow-bend of the whole body
as the brain explodes and lidless eyes
sear white. We two are bound in silence
till the pot-lid planks back and music
floods again, like a tide. Minutes later
the four of us bend to brittle pink intricate

shells, drawing white sweet flesh
with our fingers, sewing our shroud-talk
tight about us. Later, near moonless midnight,
when I scrape the leafbright broken remains
into the garbage-can outside, that last
knowing spasm eels up my arm again
and off, like a flash, across the rueful stars.

Eamon Grennan

TOTEM

All Souls' over, the roast seeds eaten, I set
on a backporch post our sculpted pumpkin under the weather,
warm still for November. Night and day it gapes
in at us through the kitchen window, going soft
in the head. Sleepwalker-slow, a black rash of ants
harrows this hollowed globe, munching the pale peach
flesh, sucking its seasoned last juices dry. In a
week, when the ants and humming flies are done, only
a hard remorseless light drills and tenants it
through and through. Within, it turns mould-black
in patches, stays days like this while the weather
takes it in its shifty arms: wide eye-spaces shine,
the disapproving mouth holds firm. Another week
a sad leap forward: sunk to one side so an eye-socket's
almost blocked, it becomes a monster of its former
self. Human, it would have rotted beyond unhappiness
and horror to some unspeakable subject state – its nose
no more than a vertical hole, the thin bridge of amber
between nose and mouth in ruins. The other socket opens
wider than ever: disbelief. It's all downhill
from here: knuckles of sun, peremptory steady fingers
of frost, strain all day and night at it, cracking
the rind, kneading the knotted fibres free. The crown
with its top-knot mockery of stalk caves in; the skull
buckles; the whole head drips tallowy tears: the end
is in sight. In a day or two it topples on itself
like ruined thatch, pus-white drool spidering
from the corner of the mouth and worming its way
down the body-post. All dignity to the winds, it bows its
bogeyman face of dread to the inevitable. And now, November
almost out, it is in the bright unseasonable sunshine
a simmer of pulp, a slow bake, amber shell speckled
chalk-grey with lichen. Light strikes and strikes
its burst surfaces: it sags, stays at the end of its
brief tether – a helmet of dark circles, death caul. Here
is the last umbilical gasp, everybody's nightmare parent,

the pitiless system rubbing our noses in it. But
pity poor lantern-head with his lights out, glob
by greasy glob going back where he came from. As each
seed-shaped drop falls free it catches and clutches
for one split second the light. When the pumpkin
lapses to our common ground at last – where a white
swaddle of snow will fold it in no time from sight –
I try to take in the empty space it's left
on top of the wooden post: it is that empty space.

Eamon Grennan

END OF WINTER

I spent the morning my father died
Catching flies. They'd buzz and hum
Against the warm illuminated pane
Of the living-room window. Breathless
My hand would butterfly behind them
And cup their fear in my fist,
Filament wings tickling
The soft centre of my palm. With my
Left hand I unlatched the window and
Opened my right wide in the sunshine.
They'd spin for a second like stunned
Ballerinas, then off with them, tiny
Hearts rattling like dice, recovered
From the fright of their lives. I watch
Each one spiral the astonishing
Green world of grass and drift
Between the grey branches of the ash.
I see each quick dark shadow
Smudge the rinsed and springing earth
That shone beyond belief all morning.
There must have been at least a dozen
I saved like that with my own hands
Through the morning, when they shook off sleep
In every corner of the living room.

Mikhail Horowitz

POEM FOR JOSEPH CORNELL

Birdman of Utopia Parkway
a perch more insular than Alcatraz
indeed your meticulous innerscapes
are tiny cells
where the fragmentary chattering of jaded parrots
a splash of color on drab walls
recalls this ghost   that guest of the memory's hospice
who came to nest a moment
& who molted with the photographs
flew the coop & dropped a quill
white as the flotsam of wonder
on the floor

Ubiquitous recluse
you walk without a body
through the missing persons bureau
of your boxes
restless & unsatisfied
looking for clues for skeleton keys
to fit the literate keyholes of your sleep
you move with the whelks
quaint relics of the sea's insomnia
with tacked-up starmaps
wheeling nowhere, wrinkled & creased
with whispers

You float from room to room
without a name without a number
a wraith who signs no register
an apparition who carries no baggage
save a luminescent soap bubble set
a sylphide souvenir case
& a cenotaph of cancelled stamps

The bright silence of these arcane coupons
shards of canaries & shed plumage of cutout cockatoos
corked bottles in the lost apothecaries
of consciousness
They call to you Joseph
they call to you from the encyclopedias of dream
the tomes of loss
from the other side of silence they call to you
your stars your stamps your toys

They long to touch you
to cancel your hands that crafted stillness
from the residue of genesis
shaped an echo in shoes & shells
& pipes no longer smoked
they call to the calcified starfish
of your fingers, still foraging for shadows
in vanishing dovecotes
they long to disassemble your scissors
cancel your hands
empty them of selection

Kiss the corks & hoops goodnight
sweet dreams to the ballerinas   the feathered pensioners
let Orion & Ondine
tuck your luminous owls over you, Joseph
let Renee Jeanmaire
soften the periwinkle you rest your head on
leave off dreaming they whisper
& go to sleep
the zodiac in the sun box the fossil fern in the analemma
will dream you
the snow soprano in the sand fountain
will dream of you always
ditto the doves & butterflies
let trade winds tousle roses in your sleep

Mikhail Horowitz

SHE SPEAKS IN TONGUES

the white,
windsoft calyx
of a dandelion seed-
head

lofted by
an olive breeze,
says

poof
& is suddenly
light's

currency,
big spender
of a butterfly

....

a distant
tractor chomps the
hay, bees

come by
& hum their day
to honey in the dust

....

& far away,
above the noon's red
sweat, the

raucous
black cicadas play
their periodic
blues

reminding us
that life is short,
& God does not speak
English

Mikhail Horowitz

SAN FRANCISCO FAUNA

Walkman scatting in Arabic
'neath a date palm spreading its hearts of gnarl
above a lunch bench, Union Square
Africans pass & European pigeons grumble
Filipino blackshirt w/coffee-colored arms
& a cocky cigarette, & here comes a couple of
Japanese dudes w/duende
&
tossing down the peopled mane of Mason,
a lioness of undetermined ethnicity
w/long red hair in a long red braid
& high heels clicking the long red lick
of her stride, to match
the macho swagger of this Mexicandelabra,
a sizzling coal-eyed, olive-
skinned Hispanic, strutting the kind of powerglide
that can only be described as,
Tai Chihuahua
&
Western businessmen in noonday glare
of suede & attache, ogling a foxy Chinese chick
in overalls, absolutely gorgeous she's
a goddamn Gang of One
&
here they all come,
delectable variations on a creamy theme,
the beautiful fruits of regnant miscegenation,
the human smoothies blended in America's melting
wok
           / Nipponese gypsies
                         Melanesian meistersingers
Irish zaddiks
                   Sicilian samurai
                                 Slavic lamas
            Finnish fakirs
                          Hebrew brujos

Celtic kahunas
                Polish picadors
                                  Bantu mandarins

      Serbo-
      Creole Hare Krishnas
      & Portuguese
      griots

Boarding the 30 bus in Chinatown
I'm the only lily
in a chattering of daffodils

Robert Kelly

THE GOSHAWKS

1.
The pleasures
of every beginning,
the lovely
fact of body,
the colors
of being difficult.

Goshawks, three, over the hill,
their white wings up there
at the edge of sight,
so high, and later
a red-shouldered hawk
lifting prey
over the excavations for
yet one more mall
just over Poughkeepsie,
just over the weather.

2.
The bird is lying. You can tell
by the rainbow pattern round the eyes –
I traded my love for this seductive glance
whose magic glamor – grammar –
spells me still. I can't
stop looking. The bird
is lying. Her arms
are white as I look up,
crucified against the sky
in the posture named Predator
Searching the Earth for What to Eat,

sky lion, the girl
soaring over the bleakness of my mind,
later, the lie that every word is lying,
the word I heard
exhausted me.
The bird is lying. Her lawyers
croaked at me from every tree,
smiled cajoling from the sun's disk
face, faced me
with their endless accu-
sations of I love you,

Pindar, poem-faker,
cloud-shaker, do-it,
dickcissel, cheese-borer,
earth-treader, sore-foot
you diet swami, you
grease from axles, charnel music,
bird-fodder, dust-devil only,
you me.

3.
Looking up, we saw six wings
one whiter than the next.

They did wheel, and silent turn
around a fix'd point no man could see

but was their primary,
their spoken word, their king. Their food.

4.
Around this center
we also move.
The prowl.
Around the food.
How white
the skin is
beneath your arms,
and on the underside of mine too
white against the sky
of what we do. All birds
are lying as they fly,
lie against the sky,
all foods are poison,
all earth the sea,
this air is fire
that we breathe and die.

The bird
(you could tell
by the rainbow light around its wings
a mile above), the bird
was lying, we had seen them
screaming like bats out of the casemate caverns
in the cliffs of Luxembourg, mesas
north of Winslow, windows
of empty Harlem brownstones,

today the sky was lying,
folks had been out for some sun
and none too cold,
sixpacks and AM, pick-ups
parked by the toilets,
men at the picnic
tables sitting, loud,
their women standing
poised to be of service when required,
attired in tight jeans, precisely
laughing, with red hair
but the sky was lying.

Anything you describe
is one more lie,
the ink can glisten in the sunlight
and still write nonsense,
still write the base
exaggerations of a heart
too scared to live forever.

5.
Where did it happen
that the bird, flying
over the nimble pastures
could look down and behold
writhing out of spring's release
an early serpent, and fall
down the pastures of the air to seize
and carry in its beak away,
where do they go, this poor
dangling surprised by dying beast, the bird
like a coolie with his string of cash
flew to his mother in the heart of the sky,

mama I found this Mexico I found this rock
this flag this heartbreak
this
    but then from the babbling beak
the snake released did fall
from the heart of the sky
back to the mud alive
and hid again inside the planet we call our own.

6.
The bird is lying you can tell by the cloud the blue
surrounding, the sky is lying
the girl came up for supper she stole a cookie
the light is lying, the sky
is dying, it is the evening and it teaches Greek,
the food is simmering in the cauldron of the heart,
the soup, the things that are dying
fall from the heart of the sky. Against
the shuddering underbelly, salmon red now from what going down,

the birds, all three of them
are diving
out of sight into the lie of darkness, the huge
imposture of the night
which nothing ends, all satisfactions are the same,
the lie that tumbles forward towards the lie of morning.

Steven Lewis

THE PONY EXPRESS RIDER REMEMBERS '88

At first the trail was hot, dust of fire
in my mouth, the ambiguous sun
making wet leather
of my craning neck.

By the time the dust settled
I looked back, the sky
the color of bloodless vengeance,
the splash of a puddle, cold

and bleak as an English moor, melting
snow splattered on my knees, dizzying
hallucinations of glory and grandeur
taken and surrendered

in the shivering hours before light,
the horror of the next dawn, a brown bottle
in my leather bag, the ache
of lovelessness in men echoed

by women everywhere, their cries
like silver coyotes across a muddy river,
nine or ten horses from horizon
to horizon and still not there.

I have taken in my leather bags
all their best intentions,
their loneliness and despair,
their earnest desire for love,

for news that will connect them
to their swirling pasts,
for the word that will make all words
disappear in the beckoning hands

at each horizon, slipping ahead
even as I remember back. They have waited
patiently for me to come, looking
out windows at the changing weather,

waiting for a storm of dust
to break the Elysian calm,
a sign they have waited long enough,
that freedom is at hand.

They have grown me
in their fertile minds
as a blossom
and then even a peach;

and near the end, a blinding ache
in my side, the weight of me
lowering their heads
like wearied branches, they watch

my cloudless arrival, they see me
dropping from the horse, laying
spread-eagled in long thick grasses,
staring blindly into the red sky,

imagining them as a child might do, biting
into the yellow flesh,
hands full and then
dripping with relief, tossing

the pit over the fence
into the next pasture
where a fresh horse blossoms
next in the midnight sun.

Steven Lewis

BAYOU GRACE

for Elizabeth

It is there because you are:
a parishioner's island, afloat
in the middle of a dark-eyed bayou,
shallow and warm (imagine a white rowboat,

paint chipping, tethered to a dock,
smooth planks leading to a live oak
of unspeakable age that spreads out
under the sun and its own shade,

Spanish moss, lifted in the breeze
like wedding lace, drifting
down toward a bed of lush
grasses flattened in your form).

It is always there.
It is there always.
It was there in the moan
of your conception.

It is there in the howl
of your hunger.
It is there in the floating dream
of voices and hands and breasts.

It is there
when you run
from the incisors of death
like a squealing rabbit.

It is there
when you bite
into the pomegranate skin of a lover,
juice dribbling down your chin.

It is there as a lover
to take your terrified arms from yourself
and lay you down
in the soft grasses of restful insignificance.

It is there as a martyr
to take the sacrosanct weights
from the rustling scales of sacred
and profane. It will be there

when the earth spins off its forsaken axis.
It will be there when your arms hurt,
when your ribs sting,
when you fall from grace

to grace.
It is there. It is you.

Steven Lewis

"IT'S NOT FAIR"

      The drifts
of snow along Franklin Avenue
remind me that even
in Currier and Ives
towns like this

the cold wind washes through
everyone, regardless of where
we live – or shop –
or dine – or who
we sleep with – or how many
people wave as we run
from the Grand Union to
Larry's Deli. The ruddy cheeks

on the boy on the cover
of an old Saturday Evening Post
are red
because he is cold;
not because he is wholesome,
or happy,
or because Jesus Christ is his
personal savior. He is alive;

not rewarded;
not punished;
in time he may forgive
the biting wind, the blinding
snow that darkens towns like this one.

There is no other way home.

David Matlin

WHEELER'S PEAK

So that there was a time when knocking on
the door a man blew the balls off another
point blank with a shotgun and the shooter
walking away got shot himself and lay dead
on the front lawn for the whole of a
morning and in the grammar of refusals that
comes with time a letter telling the tale
of doubts so that once placed in a combat ready
unit there would be no turning back
and ordered to guard an ammunition dump
the moment will come when with another shotgun
you will have to kill and in the inflammation
of that blast drive the 300SL over
what's left of the plains and ride a horse
with such deftness that the eloquence of
the father who nearly gets hanged gets
forgotten and the giant library of the
occult of the mother stuck on the plateau
in the desert gets silenced in the jaws
of the cowboy whose parents got scalped
in Cheyenne gambling gambling and
at night driving the fuel injected Pontiac
the sky suddenly turns bright as day
by the meteorite showers.

David Matlin

STONE FOREHEAD

He was on a mountain
and except for the feathers there
there was nothing. No sky
no rocks but to go on naming the names
of things that make us feel warm
in our bodies would be sad
for he was happy looking up
or looking down the feathers
he said come
and for this he must wait.
Sleep feather sleep he said rise owl
hop frog spider swim
each letter of the name
and each thing the name does
will become a comet
and wander. And in the dreams of the wanderer
fall these feathers.
I too am from a warm place
he said
and here the sky will become no color
and the ground sprout no plant
and I for these feathers walk this mountain
because they are the songs of a journey
of living things. Call him three funerals
and from him
name procession and festivals of bumblebees.
Mudsling for the headstrong.
Magpies to be slapped.

David Matlin

Bruce Brown was narrating and producing surfer
films – showed them in local Southern California
high school auditoriums – Hobie Alter – Dewey
Weber – Methedrine so's you could get down
tune your Chevy real good maybe take it to the
winternationals at Pomona and demonstrate
Newton's Second Law by way of dragstrip physics
major surgery on 18th Century mathematics how
an apple gets to be a techno spec
in terms of a do it yourself approach
and yet allowing for a certain amount of slip
hard to accept at first but perfect
for the aftermarket alarm that grows on you
in no time – the robes of Thich Quang Duc
soaked with gasoline flames eating him
and his clothes somewhere inside of June 1963
in a Saigon intersection – the Buddhists at that
moment got a head start on Andy Warhol –
the way the charred body just leaned over
and fell from its Lotus position – he became
the chief insurance for American television
coverage – the other priests kept his heart
for display in a glass case and it became
a foremost mystery American policy hasn't yet
been able to resolve.

Bruce McClelland

MONA LISA & THE DUTCH MASTER

For Pam & Theo van Groll

Enigma of her subtle framed happiness
& the dark nobility of the architect
Aristotle in contemplation: hand
on Homer's head, he thinks
to marry her. Mona Lisa
                      feels this thought

& smiles: the future, she knows,
an Italian vista, or the umber glow
or gold beneath the Rembrandt surface.
Marriage, they believe, like life.

Life, they believe, will be a series
of transformations of this theme:
Rembrandt becomes Vermeer, frames
become a house, Europe becomes
America, two becomes one.

So into his house, somber but
for him & what he remembers
of the hero stories heard as a boy
& the mature chain of understanding
golden around his neck, she brings
a complex light, a kooky smile.
He puts on some jazz.

Now they have music & light enough
for any wedding, the architect
                      imagining marriage

imagines the ship he has been building
all this time
            all this time
                      to take him home

to her, Penelope, Pamela. He smiles.
Contemplated Odysseus becomes Anyman
capable of building ships &
sailing home to Her.

Mona Lisa becomes the artist of the
Mona Lisa, her smile becomes
creation, the history of framed space filled
depicted as understood, behind her.
Into her own frame, she brings herself
in silhouette, pulling a reluctant goose
to market,

& she will someday soon, she knows,
cook for him, that quiet thoughtful man
who listens to her & likes her
complicated smile.

Bruce McClelland

FALL

A leaf a second my daughters
use their time to leave me
so wise   theories of the dry tree
– that family – drift into being.

Not lore. I wish it were.
Rather the gold of the harsh
crow caw, warning
here is morning & a man
stepping out onto his porch
not his field of fodder
before him.

All the little kernels
have been taken up
as tiny suns, in their stead,
dry sunless orphans,
loud complaint of the birds
in back.

      In black. NOT theory.
Every year those purposeful sisters
sing the praises of their loss
even as they fall.

Bruce McClelland

for A. J. Cervantes

Came riding up, Quixote,
Duende, came up with the moon
from New York, came East
against the sun, man of
memory, brief, magic.

"What do I need," he asks,
"under this tree? Where am I
everyone so young –
you & I go so far back,
as, oh, that moon."

Oh that moon. Your one good eye,
but two of us a history, world
women came into
like mist over the corn.

Came riding up.
"Am I your wife?" he asked,
eye on the stars,
from when
we were young, girls came
upon us like cascades
down a garden slope.

What marriage not to flee?
What death, that sword,
those windmills, the horse
Thunderbird. Call me Sancho.
The enemies are real.

Riding up with gold
in the saddlebags until there was
a town he could rest in,
Are you my friend? he will ask
himself, am I lost?

We are lost, my friend,
without her. When she is away
see windmills, the moon
and think of her, our chance,
her golden hair – & is she there?

Here, my friend.
You & I have been asleep
under this tree, branches creaking
in the wind. She smells of citrus
& olive, comes walking up.

"You crazy boys" she says
to wake us. It was a dream
we had, the sun imagined,
so bright we thought
we were lost.

We were each an eye
& could fix our origin.
You dreamed what I dream,
Her, the fruity scent entering
consciousness, Her a midday mirage
where only you & I are real.

That isn't true.
Whatever do we see in each other?
A small figure waving to us
in the light of our eyes.
Our tracks recede, & there she stands,
exactly where we left.

Michael Perkins

WALKING IN VERMONT

Time pursues me in this bright
Winter landscape, where the cold
Wind makes the tall trees creak.
Soon there will be forty-five
Years in my footsteps, and not
Likely another forty-five to come.
Somehow I've lived my life twice,
Survived regret – and not in vain.
I walked among the living
Gratefully, seldom in a rush,
As I hope to walk among the dead.
Time pursues me on a winter
Afternoon, and the years rise up;
But I could walk all day.

Michael Perkins

TRAIL CREW

We climbed uphill all morning
Whacking waist-high fiddlehead ferns
With swizzles, snap-cutting
The young striped maples that grow
Beside the path that winds up Lost Clove.
On one shoulder the ranger carried
A chain saw that leaked gasoline
Down his back. He cut fallen trees
While the rest of us cleared trail
Behind him, singing and telling jokes.
The July sun shimmered down through
The pine canopy and laid
A path of light past six deer
To the beaver pond below
Bellayre Mountain, where we put down
Our tools and swam naked, six strangers,
In the ice-cold green mountain water.

Michael Perkins

WINTER EVENING ON OHAYO MOUNTAIN

Snow has fallen every day this week.
Darker and softer than spilled ink,
Night catches in the icy trees
And white clouds kneel to visit
The mountain as wisps of fog.
I walk in the middle of the road,
And strangers passing in cars
Give me names I'll never hear.

Shirley Powell

HUDSON RIVER

The Hudson is like silk
caught by the cinch of bridge.
Ships rend
her seamless reaches.

Your eyes discover me,
                your hand
is like a whisper on my cheek.
Our closeness is the ride of river
on the thrust of shore.

As land becomes river,
                you
become me.
The Hudson slows,
building islands.

Its hunger for the stop of land
is like the hot ache
tangled in my legs
for your sweet flesh.

I know your gestures, every glance
from long ago
when this river first folded its deep sheen
across the searching nakedness
                of land.

Shirley Powell

AT THE BAR

It was one of those nights
    when I was standing at the bar
    I saw a man bring his hallucination in

It sat beside him (next to me)

He didn't buy it a drink
    but patted it from time to time
    when it seemed restless
Just one more beer and we'll go home
                      he said

A shadow seemed to grow there
I saw a tear fall on the bar
Wait here he told it and went back
            to the men's room

I watched it for him
After a while I touched its hand
And that was the beginning
            the edge
                of all the rooms
                that I keep going through

Shirley   Powell

THERE IS A SPHINX

There is a sphinx sitting on my desk
  paws folded lemon eyes filtering light
The sphinx has not smiled or spoken
Sometimes in the night it will
sing without moving its mouth

It is telling me something
inside the hard rind of my dreams

Its stone will grow fur here
when its sides begin wrinkling
in and then out
I will catch its breaths
  in quartzite
build it a moonpool
under my bed where
it can study its face

William Pitt Root

LATE TWENTIETH CENTURY PASTORAL

Not far from Belsen the countryside
is forgetful and kind,
senile and green.

The air is clear as a natural's conscience.

Pastures are plotted out
like stamps in an old album so vast
only a pilot inclined to glance down
might appreciate its pattern.

Those on the ground require
sealed boots to inspect
fields in the flood plains.
Viewing them through binoculars
you might startle a moment
at the sight of farmers walking on water,
plodding like cattle.

The cattle graze unattended
– munching the tallest stalks,
sloshing about,
swishing their tails and swinging
their spiritual heads to and fro,
mooing as if they bore
the griefs of the world on their bones,
their eyes a constant reference
to those sufferings
none can name.

The river that meanders there,
flushed back and forth
by floods from north and south,
gathers up flotsam and jetsam
– weeds here, sheafs of bark there –
hanging it up on barbed wire.

When eventually it cures
it is natural paper,
crude imperfect parchment,
sunbleached and rainbeaten,
where certain indigestible
fragments stubbornly
scrawl out the random glyphs
and tentative ciphers
cattle come upon in
their harmless ritual
testing of the fences.

They do this year after year,
flood after flood,
each ripening herd
bunched and huddled against
new rainfall, nibbling
a passage from
one text or another, lifting
the drooling magnificence
of heads stuffed
with scriptures assembled
by the flood.

And how inscrutably
they low
before the rainbow,
that tireless witness
their masters more knowingly
dismiss, one foot
in a pot of gold,
the other
god knows where.

William Pitt Root

THE HOUSE YOU LOOKED FOR

1.
Upstate New York,
    that haunts me still – beginning
our late fall walk in fields of blown gold weeds
and trees blown red and gold.

That time, that trip to your old home,
I saw you young, heard stories of you young as me,
your knickers stuffed with stolen cookies,
booty to share with kids you fought the day before,
the year you spent in bed, the several months
of dying you lived through.

I was proud and frightened.
You frightened me and made me proud
of what I might become, being your son.

One trip north
and our drive in country so much changed
you couldn't find for hours the place
you'd come for us to find.

2.
And now it's merely light wind,
    the long light late in the day,
weeds giving way before you,
    I in your wake in the fields,
seed fastening to my pantlegs, your legs
thrashing free of burrs and the thorns and branches
I was trapped by, you against the sun, you tall
as trees, you graceful with your earned strength moving freely.

Then, in a stand of trees the colors of fire,
the house you looked for: sagging roof, broken door
so jammed you had to force it down
with the whole forest looking on
and I looking on.

Inside, cobwebs everywhere. Antique windows
made the light antique as I heard you dressing upstairs
and your mother downstairs calling you
and down the stairs you came.
The stairs collapsing now at the house's center.

3.
Father, you could dance
and you learned to dance
with pain. They told you
you couldn't walk again.

Young and sure to die,
you lay and wept, wasting
in the bed of a closed room.

Then changed.
                    Changed
with such fierce strength
that curse become command.
You lived despite them all.
You rose, you walked, by god
you danced back into life.

I still cry when I hear
how, pale and agonized,
you made them watch you dance.
They did not understand.
You called it dance
and dancing it became.

4.
I will learn that from you.
Your eye's blue fire burned
with how I came to be.

How true you were, and strong
and how suddenly gone.

I will redeem your blood.

I promise you your name.

William Pitt Root

UNDER THE UMBRELLA OF BLOOD

In the shower not ten minutes ago and blind from the vinegar
 rinse
I was thinking 40, I'm 40
when the stinging reminded me how Turks used to bet on
just how far a headless man could run.
                              It was orderly, in its way,
with a band of selected prisoners, troops in attendance, distance
 markers,
the executioner with his two-handed sword and another man
 holding
a hammered copper plate glowing solar at the end of a pole;
as the prisoners one at a time ran past the sword took off their
 heads
and the plate scorched the neck-stumps shut to keep blood
 pressure up
so the runners ran farther, each stumbling on under the
 umbrella of blood
until the disfigured collapse, all legs and loose elbows.

Do you suppose as each head fell staring and revolving
that it could hear the tossed coins clink on the outspread
 blanket?
Could it see the body running off without it?
As it lay speechless, facing dirt or the sky, as chance would
 have it,
would it know whether it won or lost for its learned critics?

I wonder, and I rush off to the typewriter wiping my eyes clear,
knowing is I am to get it right
the images under the final downpour must be running
faster than the applauding coins of the world can ever fall.

Jan Zlotnik Schmidt

THE EDGE OF DELIGHT

Am I
an Appalachian woman
not a young girl from Brooklyn
granddaughter of a Hester Street peasant
who in the thirties
boiled cabbage chopped potatoes
to feed open mouths
Now I see women in the market
the A & P in Richmond, Kentucky
buying gizzards pigs feet pork butt
boiling scraping down meat
to feed mouths pitched open
like tiny sparrows
the women's fingers
birds' claws scratch rock
to find water
sorghum grain honey
I know these women

I too pare myself thin
wear my hands by my side
bony straight
I too feel the thrust of
jaw and cheekbone against the wind
press my fingers together
pinch the air for treasure
I too purse my lips
chop potato onion into fine little bits
I too feed open mouths

And like them
I conserve gestures
hoard my pleasure too
in the midst of despair
I savor the bare minimum
the lush green sproutings of spring
my child's springy pull on my skirt
my husband's smile a dream in daylight

Not accustomed to ask for more
I relish morsels
cooked by my own hand
as these women would
biscuits corn bread
strawberry jam
I stew fruit dried and curled
until pears prunes apricots
burst blossoming
in bubbles of water
I prepare a meal
as these women would
a peasant at a royal table.

Then after the meal
I rock sip tea
my fingers circling
the rim of the teacup
"You've got to know that edge."
Is that what these women
Would say?

Jan Zlotnik Schmidt

MEMORY:
THE PRINCESS AND THE PEA

I roll the rock
over the palm of my hand
ready to give it to you, my son,
as if it is a rare gift,
black-speckled and rust,
smooth and cold,
I roll the rock around my fingers
like a sucking candy around my tongue.

This rock brings back the summer and the sea
and salty days
our bodies curling in the sand
and sand curling between our toes.

But memory works in other ways.
I wonder what memories
will I give you,
what times will we share
that will waken you in the night
that will make you roll in your bed of down
and wonder what is stirring in your bones.

What times will I give you
What times will we share
that will make you arise
aware of the small rock of memory
at the base of your spine
destroying the sleep of your life

destroying the sleep of our lives.

Jan Zlotnik Schmidt

EVA AND JAMIE KNEW

My heart was like a wing
Eva said

and Jamie knew
Eva didn't know
what a heart
a wing was
anyhow

And all Eva said
was when I hit that bed
his muscles
next to mine
that smile
floating above me
like a cloud
I wish
my heart was like
a wing
I'd take flight
never come home

and Jamie knew
Eva never hit that high
for he ran
around quicker than
a rooster in a barn
after a spell of
lightning
he just ran and ran

but she could think
all she want
about how her heart
was like a wing
she could think and think

life just took a spell
when light fell into dust
or dust fell into light
like dandelion puffs
and down spilled
out of pillows
like clouds

life just took a spell

Pamela Uschuk

RUINED HONEY

Tonight, blurry via satellite,
a woman runs with her baby across
Hamra Street. Machine-gunned,
her back stains with orange-sized wounds.
On videotape, she jerks in yellow dust.
What is not seen is that
those slugs draw a skewer of blood
between mother and child.
What is not seen
is that morning, when hearing her baby laugh,
the woman dipped her forefinger
in honey, then rubbed her child's lips
to make laughter come again.

On the evening news, Israeli bombs
slam Beirut's ashes into the sea.
           The camera holds the stunned
faces of girls who are burst
by mortar fire, then fire.

It's a short clip
we're lost to.
What is not known is that these girls –
who would learn to smoke cigarettes in another country,
           or, who in America
might play baseball in designer jeans –
these girls, flirting,
may have stopped to joke with a jewelry vendor
then heard, above the silver
jangling, the whoomph, crack
and boom of artillery
exploding their homes on the next street.

                Maybe they thought they were lost,
smoking street transformed
into craters cradling smouldering bodies;
thought they were lost until
they saw the neighbor woman carry
her baby toward them,
warning them through the dust.
It's deceptive as a war movie,
but if once we'd seen
those dark women brew white coffee
from orange blossoms, perhaps saving
some petals to crush
like perfume into their skins
waiting to be loved, then the bullets
might rend our hearts,
                            then their burning daughters,
their dying sons could shock us,
shock us like honey suddenly
ruined on a baby's lips.

Pamela Uschuk

AUTUMN ECLIPSE

for Regina and Haig

Even behind the slush of clouds, you know
the moon is full. Your heart
is a familiar well the world falls through.
No wind sweeps night but walnut fronds
drop like cardboard wings to earth.
You remember a fondness for sunny stumps,
the lonely smell of lightning-felled trees,
a clearing in the woods
where you picked Bergamot
and Forget-Me-Nots that wilted before dusk came.
Everything is going fine,
no hitches, just middle age.
Now, in the sad amphitheatre of sky, bear
and swan disappear and what you hear
is the swamp attended by a gushing flume.
You might mistake a shadow for a bittern
with its head thrown back, camouflaged
by upthrust reeds.
Everything radiates white light,
is a quick ghost of itself,
even your feet, kicking through
memory, the unbidden leaves falling from dream,
the still-green stalks of lilies gone to seed,
raspberry bramble, cranberry bog,
lamb's tongue, goldenrod, slabs
of wet blue slate
to the glaciated land you grew up with.
Then, you see again the sudden owl,
eyes red spears,
brown wings on fire, trailing sparks
into the dry woods the day you became a woman.
Bloody coals blew to flame.
You can feel the moon, the shadow
of your own earth pulling across

its broad silver palm.
Even treefrogs cease their harmonic thrum
while geese oboe south
through the echoing sky until there is nothing
but the empty cover of your skin, softening.
More manic in this silence,
the flume bursts its course
and you laugh at the mechanics of fate,
the way, no matter how far you travel,
you always come back to this – the world
swallowed gradually by dark,
its dramatic recovery of light.

Pamela Uschuk

WITH ITS TOLL OF CHAR

All sounds bassoon in haze.
Trees stretch shoulder deep
in fog breathing up from the slow river
where the courting of frogs booms
under the moon's waning halo.
To vague stars turning over sky, black limbs
hold up their devotion of autumn leaves.
Inside midnight's sleeve, the architecture
of imagination slips
from its routine mooring
in an earthquake of dream, and I think
of the car jarring you awake
as I skidded to miss the fox
sniffing its mate dead on the freeway.
What shapes irony? Coming home late
from the city after the Laureate's story
of the fox-faced man who peeked
at him from the kitchen door, then places
his charred hands over his poems,
I started at the overwhelming red tail
as it brushed the rushing front bumper.
The fox was real.
In winter, you said, it's too dangerous
to swerve for animals caught on the ice.

Event becomes myth. How often we drift,
safe in our faith something will
get us home alive, even when
we risk everything. Even inspiration
or love is subject to killing flames.
Night gathers details
we forget. What it says comes true.
Even in fog,
frogs never give up
their insistent courting and stars
chart careful courses to dawn.
Sometimes we need most
fire that could destroy us,
flame that becomes its own fuel,
charging the heart with its toll of char.

In the unkempt church of desire
we make choices to keep out
or bring us to storms.
I can't forget that fox, how he must have watched
his mate cross the pavement
like a stream parting their known woods
in the nightly routine of their hunt.
What he couldn't name
split her side, flipping her once
as he snapped at the monstrous shape
even as it was swallowed wholly by dark.
The fox might have started sooner
from the car but he stood
sniffing her a last time,
that commonplace night none of us
could any longer take for granted,
as his red fur ignited, guard hairs
flaming spikes.

Janine Vega

AMERICAN ARTISTS

My friends and I sat on the
picnic table
we talked about how the world was
how we wanted it to be
the table was slanted
we ate our lunch
a cold air running through our fingers

who knows about the farms inside
the ones we carry around
– if the crops are gathered
or the well is dry
or the roots
wrenched out of the earth?
we sat together and ate our lunch

half revealed in the gray light
were the stones of ourselves, our bones
and molars, none of us were fat
nor clearly defined
lines wavered about the chin as the roads
composed themselves
and the landscapes settled

an element of fear sat in the scarred
photographs, the torn posters
and revelatory dreams
a complicity of misery in the gnarled
hands of sharecroppers, migrant workers
exiles born out of a country
no one saw any more

then, like a wind buried in the tree line
that comes singing over the heads
of the farmers a forgotten tune
someone laughed
we all laughed
we jumped up and down on the table
the farms followed us home.

Janine Vega

BELTANE

Hay fires roll down dragon hill
the strolling planets in
single file
stars above us, stars below us
three times around the pillar of stone
three times around the well
we follow the sun

Thrust of peas, garlic, onion grass
old iron in the fields bereft
stone ardor of buried cold
in the spears of crocus, iris, daffodil
the arching foot of jonquil
at attention

Battered coat of ravenous deer
cropping bright green mosses
the white-tailed rabbit leaps
four feet in the air
trillium opens at the mouth of a cave
by the fiddlebow, wild onion

Mating woodpeckers hammer on
live trees, loud, insistent
crones wait for warm hands, watching
as the plow goes in
you are old, old
the kind and the queen meet
once again.

Janine Vega

FOR THE MASTER SINGER

The elements separate, Johann Sebastian
and I run to the cliffs with small steps
drinking in

sea sky water mist
and sweat on the shoulders

the elements separate, Johann Sebastian
and falling on one's knees
is not enough

no, not enough in the times we live in
light clothes, walking shoes
like the poets of our days
wandering through catacombs,
cathedrals, certain of echoes
directing us

to go out at midnight
Johann
is not enough

We need, despite the tenderness of earth
for our bodies
lavender wind, translucent air
that plucks the feathers of our drunken
crewcut and leaves us helplessly exposed
the flame-headed child

I have also lapped at the bowl
of the all forgiving
much work to be done, sang the waves
I could hardly contain myself
the baptismal font ran red
with desire
the young man and I leaned languidly
over, convinced it was blood

What never changes, Johann
is desire
sweet desire
knows its name is written on doors
and runs eagerly to find
what church what well
what holy font will give me?

Give me, sings desire
sweet desire
give me or I'll die
knees skin and eyes sing
take me
sensate elemental mother
font of waters take me
here I am.

Janine Vega

LITTLE GHOST IN THE STATION

(For Richard Manuel)

Looking through the window down the track
to the north, she peeled a piece of plastic
from the pane
the birds would have a hard time of it
tonight, the frozen wind, the waves
looping and crashing on the rocks,
especially the migratory ones,
the white-throated sparrow who had just
appeared in the courtyard yesterday
and sung his heart out

The plastic scraping rose in the draft
from the track below
and she thought of her mother
her mother who thought of birds
on the fiercest mornings, and threw
them bread with bacon drippings,
The plastic fluttered up again,
a tiny dybbuk in the window corner,
a tiny message from her mother,
a voice in the phone from far away

She worried about the birds, too
especially that one, God's flute player
who gave her spring at the fire escape
when she whistled and he answered
the same four notes he sang in the Catskill
summers when she reached a peak
"Poor John Is Dead," he sang
and now it was winter, quiet at the window,
and she did not need a cigarette
she needed to weep.

Irving Weiss

THE DEAD TAKE ADVANTAGE

Dead as they were we could still detect movement.
They were indeed dead but we sensed the tiny alterations
the barely perceptible
tremors, flutters.
Not that we felt free to tell each other about them
let alone announce the fact baldly
nor even admit anything to ourselves
(not even I admit to myself wordlessly)
about faint signs and suspicions
a flaccid cheek that had quivered there
or an exhausted eyelid trembling here.
Who could say? But we were sure we knew.

And then in the darkness before dawn
the dead sprang up
and ran shrieking like Banshees down the hill
eyes rolling
flames zigzagging in all directions from their hideous naked hides
as they spooked the night watchmen
blighted the house plants, backed up the septic tanks
and then fell on the sleeping inhabitants
raping men, women, and children alike
hard and unmercifully
without waking them
before they ran shrieking up the hill again
to lie motionless down
justifying our conviction at the last
that they had really been moving ever so slightly before.

Irving Weiss

THE INSECTS ARE CRAWLING ON THE FACE OF THE DAY AFTER TOMORROW

Where are the cats?
They are roaming, looking for birds.
Where are the birds?
They are flitting from tree to tree.
Where are the cats now?
They are climbing the trees, surely, looking for birds.
And the birds?
They are flitting from branch to branch.
Why don't the birds fly away?
They are hungry, they are looking for insects among the leaves.
The cats are motionless in the branches now.
The leaves are cat-faced.
The insects crawl over the untwitching hides of the cats waiting for birds.
Now the birds flit deeper among the leaves.
Tomorrow the cats will be there as they are now.
The insects are crawling on the face of the day after tomorrow.

Irving Weiss

CULTIVAR, NOTHING

I almost got sick –
Princeton Nurseries, I was up there
wounding trees about a year and a half ago,
and they had this marvelous planting of Silver Linden,
Tilia tomentosa, cultivar, nothing;
but it was a butted selection,
but they had not officially
ever named it or released it.
And I guess the trees were 2.5 to 4,
somewhere in there,
caliper.

And they looked fantastic
and I knew what the mother tree looked like
or the clone originally.
And the next time I went up in that planting,
I wounded two of them. There were two trees left,
the two I had wounded.
They cut the rest of them down: 237 trees,
because no one asked for them.
Shame on them for not publicizing it.
Shame on you, in a word, for not reading through the book
and getting to *Tilia tomentosa* and saying,
"Hey, this is probably a damn site better
than *Tilia cordata.*" and it probably is.
And the interesting thing
is watching the bees die when they suck up the honey.
It's intriguing.

Nancy Willard

LITTLE ELEGY WITH BOOKS AND BEASTS

(In memory of Martin Provensen, 1916-1987)

I.

Winters when the gosling froze to its nest
he'd warm it and carry it into the house praising
its finely engraved wings and ridiculous beak,
or sit all night by the roan mare, wrapping
her bruised leg, rinsing the cloths while his wife
read aloud from "Don Quixote," and darkness hung
on the cold steam of her breath,
or spend five days laying a ladder for the hen
to walk dry-shod into the barn.

Now the black cat broods on the porch.
Now the spotted hound, meeting visitors, greets none.
Nestler, nurse, mender of wounded things,
he said he didn't believe in the body.
He lost the gander, elder of all their beasts
(not as wise as the cat but more beloved),
the night of the first frost, the wild geese
calling – last seen waddling south
on the highway, beating his clipped wings.

II.

He stepped outside through the usual door
and saw for the last time his bare maples
scrawling their cold script on the low hills
and the sycamore mottled as old stone
and the willows slurred into gold by the spring light,
and he noticed the boy clearing the dead brush –
old boughs that broke free under the cover of snow –
and he raised his hand, and a door in the air opened,
and what was left of him stumbled and fell
and lay at rest on the earth like a clay lamp
still warm whose flame was not nipped or blown
but lifted out by the one who lit it
and carried alive over the meadow –
that light by which we read, while he was here,
the chapter called Joy in the Book of Creation.

Nancy Willard

A WREATH TO THE FISH

Who is this fish, still wearing its wealth,
flat on my drainboard, dead asleep
its suit of mail proof only against the stream?
What is it to live in a stream,
to dwell forever in a tunnel of cold,
never to leave your shining birthsuit,
never to spend your inheritance of thin coins?
And who is the stream, who lolls all day
in an unmade bed, living on nothing but weather,
singing, a little mad in the head,
opening her apron to shells, carcasses, crabs,
eyeglasses, the lines of fishermen begging for
news from the interior – oh, who are these lines
that link a big sky to a small stream
that go down for great things:
the cold muscle of the trout,
the shining scrawl of the eel in a difficult passage,
hooked – but who is this hook, this cunning
and faithful fanatic who will not let go
but holds the false bait and the true worm alike
and tears the fish, yet gives it up to the basket
in which it will ride to the kitchen
of someone important, perhaps the Pope
who rejoices that his cook has found such a fish
and blesses it and eats it and rises, saying,
"Children, what is it to live in the stream,
day after day, and come at last to the table,
transfigured with spices and herbs
a little martyr, a little miracle;
children, children, who is this fish?"

Nancy Willard

HOW THE HEN SOLD HER EGGS TO THE STINGY PRIEST

An egg is a grand thing for a journey.

It will make you a small meal on the road
and a shape most serviceable to the hand

for darning socks, and for barter
a purse of gold opens doors anywhere.

If I wished for a world better than this one
I would keep, in an egg till it was wanted,

the gold earth floating on a clear sea.
If I wished for an angel, that would be my way,

the wings in gold waiting to wake,
the feet in gold waiting to walk,

and the heart that no one believed in
beating and beating the gold alive.

Nancy Willard

SAINT PUMPKIN

Somebody's in there.
Somebody's sealed himself up
in this round room,
this hassock upholstered in rind,
this padded cell.
He believes if nothing unbinds him
he'll live forever.

Like our first room
it is dark and crowded.
Hunger knows no tongue
to tell it.
Water is glad there.
In this room with two navels
somebody wants to be born again.

So I unlock the pumpkin.
I carve out the lid
from which the stem raises
a dry handle on a damp world.
Lifting, I pull away
wet webs, vines on which to hang
the flat tears of the pumpkin,

like fingernails or the currency
of bats. How the seeds shine,
as if water had put out
hundreds of lanterns.
Hundreds of eyes in the windless wood
gaze peacefully past me,
hacking the thickets,

and now a white dew beads the blade.
Has the saint surrendered
himself to his beard?
Has his beard taken root in his cell?

Saint Pumpkin, pray for me,
because when I looked for you, I found nothing,
because unsealed and unkempt, your tomb rots,
because I gave you a false face
and a light of my own making.

Howard Winn

CINDERELLA

When she sat in the ashes,
dark smudge on one cheek
and the left wrist
(she brushed a loose lock of hair
away with the back of her hand)
she felt right.
Her father's wife used to say
she should have more drive.
(She used words like that.)
The other daughters had ambition.
They wanted to marry doctors,
or lawyers, or bankers, or
rising young computer wizards
near Boston or Sunnyvale.
(The latter would be best.)
She did not care.
Fire was warm and her imagination
found pictures in flames.
She saw faces, drawing them
in thin coat of gray dust
over red tile.
One of them became real,
rising up before her,
body solidifying from smoke,
like a genie from a bottle.
It might have been a fairy godmother
or dreams personified.
"Bring me what I desire
but am afraid to say," she said.
Miniature whirlwinds danced
across the ordinary hearth
which opened as in an earthquake.
Her body, without support, fell away.
The abyss closed. Fire burned
as brightly as before.
She did not return, not even at midnight.

Howard Winn

WALLACE STEVENS ESCAPES CONNECTICUT

Settling into the car seat,
he feels his body cradled by fabric,
springs and cotton batting, all natural.
Black steel and glass surrounds
his ears and eyes. The steering wheel
is first cool to his hands. They warm it.
He drives carefully through Connecticut
countryside, leaving Hartford behind.
His velocity is constant, measured
by speedometer which he assumes correct.
Signs along the highway shoulder
instruct him in rules and standards.
He conducts himself as law abiding citizen
and does not find doing so difficult.
Dials on the dashboard inform him
the battery is being charged, engine
temperature is correct, fuel is adequate,
and oil is bathing parts under
proper pressure. This minor mechanical
universe functions.
Great shadows follow his vehicle,
skimming over gray road surface.
They seem wings trailing behind
some swan strangely without color
or absolute form. He sees them as black.
They rise from roadway and become more
than surface. Beating, they lift
him towards the sun. Is he now
Daedalus? Shedding steel and fabric
like reptile skins, he rises through morning
mists the sun itself, breaking
through birds in early flock as into glass
mirrors and beyond, Apollo riding
his fiery feathered chariot east to west,
casting black bird shadows of wings

over highways and arbitrary state lines.
Earth becomes map. He leaves it, airbound,
tied in his orbit as he arcs in red-
orange trajectory whose after-image
remains dark green, almost black
for any observer searching upward
into otherwise empty skies.

Howard Winn

MY FATHER'S OTHER WORLD

He and I did not occupy the same country.
It was the same space.
His house and land touched mine.
Grass filled the yards between
and I could not see the property line.
Cardinals called from the top of my trees.
Periwinkle spilled down my banks.
Yew, laurel, and honeysuckle spread
about the house.
Sugar maples, oaks, and hemlock
ringed the open land,
but ogres filled his forest,
long-dead dragons breathed fire
that scorched his lawn.
Bandits waylaid travelers who turned
to his door. At night, dark forms convened
upon his steps plotting vile ceremonies.
In the morning, his eyes filled with fear
and he asked if those at our house had survived.

Howard Winn

COMMERCE

The crazy dog lives at the service station,
brains disconnected by gasoline fumes and coke.
Bald tires are his friends,
smelling like alley cats.
He sleeps curled inside one
and absorbs odor of old rubber.
His tongue hangs out on hot days,
pink sponge full of flat soda.
He sniffs ankles of customers paying cash,
accepting a Planter's Peanut
purchased from automatic office vendor.
His love cannot be bought by peanuts.
He does not allow a scratch of the ears,
bowing his head away in charade of submission
that avoids intimacy with strangers.
Piles of empty oil cans are his Riviera
where he suns himself waiting perhaps
in twitching slumber for second coming
of canine millennium and dog heaven
or extinction. In his lunatic world,
no moon is as bright or clear
as orange disk of Gulf insignia.

BIOGRAPHIES

David Appelbaum is an avid bicyclist and builder of rock walls. His books of poetry include *Pointe* (Ptermigon Press, 1976), *First Stop* (Springtown Press, 1987), and *On Count* (Mellen, 1989).

Carley Rees Bogarad is currently Acting Dean of Liberal Arts and Sciences at the College at New Paltz, State University of New York. Her poems have appeared in numerous journals and anthologies. Her recent scholarship focuses on Sylvia Plath and Margery Kempe.

Audrey Borenstein, NEA Fellow and Rockefeller Fellow, has published poetry, essays and over two dozen short stories in literary magazines. Excerpts from the three novels of her trilogy-in-progress, *From the Palatine Sketch Book,* appear in *Oxalis* (Winter 1987-88), *Resoundings* (April, 1988) and in *The Albany Review* (December, 1988).

(J)ames (J)ohnston Clarke is a middle-aged Presbyterian whose idea of a good time is to sulk. He was born in Pollard Mills, Kentucky and he has taught English at Ulster County Community College for the past twenty years. He has published five chapbooks of poetry, the most recent being *The Crow Of The Moon.*

Regina deCormier-Shekerjian is a recipient of the 1984 Pablo Neruda Award (selected by Richard Howard). Forthcoming are translations of Christine de Pisan's poetry for *A Christine de Pisan Reader* (Persea Books). Among her published books, *Discovering Israel* (Random House) received a National Jewish Book Award.

Rosemary Deen is the poetry editor of *Commonweal* magazine. She's been teaching at Queens College of the City University of New York for about 25 years, having come by way of Michigan and Chicago, by studies and marriage. She began by loving writing, learning, teaching. When she was 19, a friend made her look at paintings, sculpture, buildings till she couldn't stop. In her experience loving is a good beginning because it lasts. Together with the poet Marie Ponsot, she's the author of two books on the teaching of writing: *Beat Not The Poor Desk* (which won the MLA's Mina Shaughnessy Medal) and *The Common Sense*. Together with the Blake scholar, Leonard Deen, she is the author of five children. Her book of poems is *Angels Haunt The Renaissance*.

Samuel Exler received his BA from Brooklyn College and was a dropout from the Master's program at Columbia. He has been a warehouse and kitchen worker, combat infantry soldier, print production manager, advertising copywriter; he now practices psychotherapy in Stone Ridge.

David C. D. Gansz, born in 1960, was educated at Oxford and Canterbury Universities, Bard College and The Milton Avery Graduate School of the Arts, taking degrees in theology, art history and poetry. He is the author of *Animadversions* (Logres Press, 1986). Formerly an Instructor of English and Writing at Marist College and Managing Editor of Station Hill Press, he is currently Senior Contributing Editor of *NOTUS: New Writing* magazine. He was awarded an Individual Artists Fellowship by the Dutchess County Arts Council for 1988-89.

Roberta Gould's fifth book, *Not By Blood Alone And Other Poems* (Waterside), will be released shortly. Her other books are *Only Rock* (Folder Editions), *Estanaranja* (Lince, Mexico City), *Writing Air, Written Water* (Waterside), and *Dream Yourself Flying* (Four Zoas Press). She is currently Secretary of the International Committee For The Well Being Of The People Of Mexico, which is raising first world tourist consciousness on (1) the need to tip generously when abroad, and (2) the need to ignore misinformation that encourages price haggling and the resultant perpetuation of poverty in Mexico and other touristed third world countries.

Eamon Grennan was born in Dublin in 1941. His poems have appeared in magazines in Ireland and in America. His two volumes—*Wildly For Days* and *What Light There Is*—were published (1983, 1987) by Gallery Press, Dublin. North Point Press will publish a collected volume in 1989. He was educated at University College, Dublin and Harvard, and is currently in the Department of English at Vassar College.

Mikhail Horowitz is currently arts and entertainment editor for the *Woodstock Times*. Though widely published in the small press universe, he is better known as a performance poet, working with jazz musicians and spieling in the oral tradition of

Vachel Lindsay and Lord Buckley. His book, *Big League Poets* (City Lights, 1978) is no longer in print.

Robert Kelly has "lived beside the stream Metambesen for twenty years, in terrain held by the Wappingers and the Esopus as sacred to parley and discourse, hence not much killed over. It is a land into which many poets have come, and where many have learned to take refuge in mind. The poem in this collection started as I watched three goshawks circling very high over Bowdoin Park; I thought of the apparent serenity of their passage, and then of the litigious disposition we all share, our endless quarrel over the bone, even if the bone is the immense sky." More recent work include *Not This Island Music* (poems, 1987), *Doctor Of Silence* (a second collection of short fiction, 1988), and *The Flowers Of Unceasing Coincidence* (a long poem, 1988).

Steven Lewis is married twenty years and has seven children. When domestic life allows, he is a teacher, a writer and editor of Springtown Press. In addition to two collections of poems, *Exits Off A Tollroad* and *Geographics,* and several chapbooks, his work has been seen in publications as diverse as *The Christian Science Monitor, Confrontation,* and *L.A. Parent.*

David Matlin—"The little town where I first grew up, Chino California, was filled with suspicion and hatred between helpless gangwar Pachucos and Okie millionaire potato ranchers still fresh choked by their migration from Oklahoma the memories of ten million years of top soil gone sand blast their horses and corn and children. In 1965 I moved to Detroit Michigan, got seared by the Vietnam War and the consequences of America, worked in factories, danced in 'blind pigs' and began meeting or hearing about those poets and artists who would and have offered me a lasting sense of not only the share I might have, but the fact that it lies outside any guarantee or kindness. 1970 I moved to Berkeley California then Buffalo New York and next New York City itself. I now live in Saugerties, a small town half way up the Hudson River Valley."

Bruce McClelland—Born July 6, 1949, in Chicago. Grew up in St. Louis. Educated at Bard College (B.A., Russian; M.F.A., Writing); Cornell University and University of Pennsylvania (graduate study in Linguistics); State University of New York at Albany (graduate study in Russian Literature). Currently live in Rhinebeck, N.Y. with my wife Cynthia. Author of *The Dracula*

Poems and *The Marchen Cycle,* my most recent book of poetry is *This World.* Published last year was also a bilingual edition of my translation of Osip Mandelstam's second book, *Tristia.* From my desktop in Rhinebeck, I have just started up St. Lazaire Press, a small cooperative poetry press. Other than that, I have a full time job as a designer of electronic information retrieval systems for BRS Information Technologies in Latham, N.Y.

Michael Perkins is the author of two books of poems, *The Persistence Of Desire* and *Praise In The Ears Of CLouds,* as well as a number of novels, including *Evil Companions* and *Down Here,* and a book of literary criticism published by William Morrow, *The Secret Record.* His poetry, journalism and reviews have appeared in over a hundred magazines, including *Mother Jones, The Nation, Choice, The Village Voice* and *Exquisite Corpse.* Formerly editor of *Ulster Arts* magazine, he now works as Program Director for the Woodstock Guild. He lives on Ohayo Mountain in Woodstock, overlooking the Ashokan Reservoir.

Shirley Powell grew up in Ohio and spent "hunks of time" in California and New York City before settling in the Catskills. She has taught school (every age from first grade through college freshman and also adults) in the three states, has a B.S. Ed. from Miami University (Ohio) and an M.A. in Creative Arts from New York University. She works now for Poets in Public Service, operating out of Union Square in New York City, and does freelance writing, including newspaper correspondent assignments and features. She has a published novel and two books of poems, one in two editions. Besides writing poetry and stories, she is a storyteller.

William Pitt Root's most recent collection is *Faultdancing* (Pitt Poetry Series 1986). "Under the Umbrella of Blood" is the title poem of his seventh book, for which he's currently seeking a publisher. Until coming east to direct the Creative Writing program at Hunter College, he had lived and worked mostly in the western United States. Awards include N.E.A., Rockefeller, Guggenheim, Stegner, and U.S./U.K. writing grants. He also publishes short fiction and translations. He and his wife, Pamela, live outside New Paltz with three large dogs, Mu, Drambuie, and Oscar W.

Jan. Z. Schmidt is Coordinator of the Composition Program at the State University of New York at New Paltz where she teaches Composition, Autobiography and Creative Writing courses. She has had poems published in many journals including *Cincinnati Poetry Review, River City Review, Wind, Alaska Quarterly Review, Bitterroot, The Panhandler, Appalachian Heritage, Plainsong, The Pikeville Review,* and *Kansas Quarterly.* Her work also has been featured in *The Anthology Of Magazine Verse* and *Yearbook Of American Poetry.* She views the poet as one overwhelmed by the "fullness of life"—by sense of both possibility and loss.

Pamela Uschuk's poems have appeared in *Poetry, Tendril, Pequod, The Bloomsbury Review, Arete* and others. They are forthcoming in *Ascent, The Montana Review, In Wilderness Lies Preservation* (Paris and London) and others. Last spring, she was one of the winners of the Stone Ridge Poetry Contest. Currently she teaches Creative Writing through Marist College at Green Haven Correctional Facility, as well as serves as a Poet In Public Service in New York. She lives with her husband, William Pitt Root, outside of New Paltz "at the edge of the forest."

Janine Pommy Vega is the author of *Poems To Fernando* (City Lights, 1968), *Journal Of A Hermit* (Cherry Valley Edition, 1974), *Morning Passage* (Telephone Books, 1976), *Here At The Door* (Zone Press, 1978), *Journal Of A Hermit &* (Cherry Valley Editions, 1979), *The Bard Owl* (Kulchur Press, 1980), *Apex Of The Earth's Way* (White Pine Press, 1984). Two new books in 1988 are *Aves Salvajes Del Corazon* (Wild Birds of the Heart) from Las Lluvias Press in Lima, Peru; and *Drunk On A Glacier, Talking To Flies,* from Tooth of Time Books in New Mexico. Ms. Vega lives in Bearsville, and works in New York State Poets In The Schools in New York City, and upstate New York. She was the co-founder of the Sing Sing Poetry Workshop and has been its co-director for the past four years.

Irving Weiss was formerly Professor of English, State University of New York at New Paltz. Recently he had a visual poem published in Bengali translation. Selections from his forthcoming *A Dictionary Of Childhood* were published in *The Sun* in August, 1988. He now lives in Chestertown, Md.

Nancy Willard's books of poetry include *Household Tales Of Moon And Water, A Visit To William Blake's Inn,* and *Water Walker.*

Howard Winn was born in Poughkeepsie and, after serving in the Twentieth Air Force in the Western Pacific, received his degrees from Vassar College and from Stanford University. At the latter, he was a Newhouse Scholar in the Creative Writing Program where he studied with Yvor Winters and Wallace Stegner. He has also studied at California State University at San Francisco, New York University and Middlebury College. At the latter, he worked with the late John Ciardi. He has been a social worker in California, written for Public Television in San Francisco, and taught in the schools of Petaluma, Calif. He is currently Professor of English at Dutchess Community College. His poetry has appeared on the buses of the Holyoke Street Railway Company as part of a National Endowment for the Humanities program administered by the *Massachusetts Review* to bring poetry directly to the people. His work has also appeared in such publications as *Epoch, Beloit Poetry Journal, Sparrow, Southern Humanities Review,* and *The Kansas Quarterly.*